So He Cheated, Now What?

Do I Stay or Walk Away?

Nicole Cleveland

Quality Publishing Services

Published by

DocUmeant Publishing
14 Wall St 20th Floor
NY, NY 10005

Phone: 646-233-4366

Cover designed by
DocUmeant Designs

www.DocUmeantDesigns.com

Ginger Marks,
Copy Editor & Layout by
DocUmeant

www.DocUmeant.net

To order Book Group copies or copies in bulk phone

757-404-1582

ISBN-13: 978-0-9826005-0-4 12.99
ISBN-10: 098260050X

Printed in USA

DEDICATION

I dedicate this book to Pop-Pop, Nana, Aunt Cile, Grandmom Theresa & Aunt Barbara.

You were called away too soon. If you were here I know you would be proud of me. I'm not that wild child anymore. (smile)

CONTENTS

WORDS OF PRAISE

"In a time when the media's portrait of marriage is gloom, Nicole Cleveland steps up to the call and releases a dynamic book, So He Cheated, Now What. This willing vessel of God did not hide behind a mask and pretend that everything was okay, but chose to seek GOD's face and ask why me? Nicole allowed GOD to turn even this situation around for her good, her husband's good, the good of their marriage and ultimately the many lives that will be blessed because she was transparent. Nicole, I am so proud of you for digging in deep and going to the CROSS with your questions, hurts and allowing GOD to refine NICOLE, the daughter HE CHOSE for such a time as this and with a message like this. May "So He Cheated, Now What" deliver women from the destructive mindset that work against marriage and bless those that need to know they are not alone. May God continue to bless you because you are such a blessing to others." **- Dr. Taffy Wagner, CEPF Money Talk Matters, LLC Author of Debt Dilemma www.moneytalkmatters.com**

"For such a time as this, God has blessed and poised you and your husband to be a testimony for so many couples who have gone through trials and tribulations, not only in their marriages, but even before saying, 'I do'.

Upon receiving your book, I grabbed a cup of coffee and started reading and literally did not stop until I had finished it completely! I remember shaking my head in agreement; I remember feeling your pain and saying, "Thank you Jesus," for what He had done for and with your husband. Last but surely not least, I remember saying how so many will be blessed with a real message of what couples deal with behind closed doors every single day, and how to let go and let God restore what He put together in the genesis of that relationship.

As women, we have the tendency to allow our emotions to make the final decision. We allow our friends to tell us what to do with our spouses during a challenge, but some how those friends are never around when we want to share the beautiful times.

Because of your steadfast and unwavering faith—no matter how difficult it seemed to be, you held on to God's word; for that I say congratulations! God promised to never leave you nor forsake you—just like Job, you believed Him and He restored everything back to you!

To God be the glory for the things HE has done." **- Regina Baker 'Keeping It Real' http://ReginaBaker.com**

PREFACE

"Rebuilding trust is a joint effort and begins in your mind."~ Nicole Cleveland

Nicole Cleveland knows a little something about rebuilding a marriage after an affair. Her very own marriage was almost destroyed when her husband abandoned their family a mere five days after she gave birth to their third child. After a shameful separation, the Lord restored her marriage. In the midst of her pain, she found her purpose; to encourage motivate and inspire women by sharing her personal testimony with women everywhere.

In 2006 she founded BreatheAgainMagazine.com, an online portal for women. It is a safe-haven where they can find encouragement, by reading real-life testimonies of women that have endured some of life's most challenging obstacles.

Nicole's Mission Statement: *"To offer hope and a moment of encouragement even if it's to just one woman."*

ACKNOWLEDGEMENTS

What, who and where would I be without the Lord? I thank him daily for his Grace and Mercy.

Jerry–I bless God for the relationship we have today. It had to happen so that God could get the Glory from the restoration. Thank you for letting me tell my story. It takes a real man to allow his "wrongdoings" to be in the open for the entire world to see. When I am in my office you keep the kids busy and I love you for that. I hear you sometimes whisper, "Don't bother Mommy, she's working on Breathe Again." You understand the mission and you are my #1 supporter. I will love you forever!

Tevan–My handsome, powerful Man of God–I believe in you and can see what you can't see. I will love you forever!

Felicia & Nichelle–Thank you for allowing Mommy to do what I do and letting me "play" on the computer. I love you forever.

Mom–You are my #1 fan. I saw you work and clean other people's houses so that we could have. Thank you. I love you forever.

Pastors Cliff & Vicki Coward–Thank you for your prayers.

Corrie – The best Virtual Assistant in the world. Thank you for all that you do. It is appreciated.

A huge thank you goes out to Ginger for helping me put this book together. You have the patience of Job and I thank you for that.

To my very 1st readers - Linda Dominique Grosvenor, author of "The Plural Thing" and Dr. Taffy Wagner author of "Debt Dilemma" - Your feedback lit a fire under me and I am so thankful that you took time out of your schedule for me and my 1st book. (love ya)

To all the readers and subscribers of Breathe Again Magazine, thank you for your unwavering support and believing in us. I do what I do for you and the millions of women that have no voice—women that are suffering in silence. Someone, somewhere, knows how you feel. They made it and so can you. *I made it and so can you.* Stay Blessed

INTRODUCTION

After all we'd been through, taking my husband back was the easy part; rebuilding trust was much harder.

In January 2005 my husband and I reconciled. I told myself that I would *never* take him back if he cheated again, especially if he got her pregnant. But to tell the truth, I have learned "*never say never*"–especially when God has the final say.

I remember telling my mother-in-law that the chapter of my life with her son was over, and that I was closing that chapter forever. Now, my husband's mother is one of those "Church Of God In Christ" (COGIC), older, hat-wearing, sanctified, mothers of the church, who also happens to be an Evangelist. She is sweet as peach cobbler, but don't mess with her "in the spirit." She calmly said in a very soft whisper, *"But did God say the chapter was over? Until He says it's over, it ain't over baby."*

"Goodbye Mom," I said as I hung up the phone.

Many of our conversations ended that way. She had a way of telling me what I didn't want to hear. And it always seemed to come at the wrong time. She would even call me at five in the morning, pray for me, and end with the phrase, *"Thus saith the Lord, and it is done"*. Then she would just hang up. Thinking back on that day makes me smile, because I have learned that again–it's not about me.

I know I obeyed God when I agreed to reconcile, but was I ready for the journey that I was about to embark on? It has been two years, and I am just now becoming truly free. It does not happen overnight. It is a process.

"I am free... Praise the Lord, I'm free... No longer bound... No more chains holding me.... My soul is resting.... It's just a blessing.... Praise the Lord Hallelujah I'm free..."

Twenty four years ago a high wired teenager declared to her cousin David that one day she was going to write a book.

Today it is a reality. That teenager was me.

- Nicole Cleveland

CHAPTER I

THIS WAS NOT IN THE PLAN

Fall in love, get married, stay in church, have kids–that was the plan. Most women marry with the thought that their marriage will survive "until death do you part." That is the vow we take. Do we really understand the complexity of that statement?

Back to the Plan

Get married, have kids, and go to church on Sunday, was my plan. Most couples say, if you get past the first five years, you are good to go. Your marriage will last forever. Yippee! So, what happens when it starts to fall apart after 7, 10, 15 or even 24 years? People are divorcing every day after 20+ years of marriage. This has to stop!

Getting married for all the wrong reasons

√ He is fine

√ His body is bangin'

√ He's got money

√ He's got benefits

√ I'm pregnant

√ I need a daddy for my kids

√ He goes to church

√ He makes me feel good

Why did I get married?

"I married to have a driver so I could take my business on the road."

"I married because he had potential."

"I married for security."

We all do it–male and female, black or white. Those physical and /or emotional attractions are very important, but it should not *seal the deal*. And it is a deal–it's an agreement between <u>three</u> parties that *come-hell-or-high-water*, I am here to stay.

We cover each other. *"I gotcha back."* And please, please, please, do not look for your man in the church. Remember we ALL are there to be delivered from something.

When I say *three parties,* I truly mean it. No, it's nothing freaky, but it is a threesome.

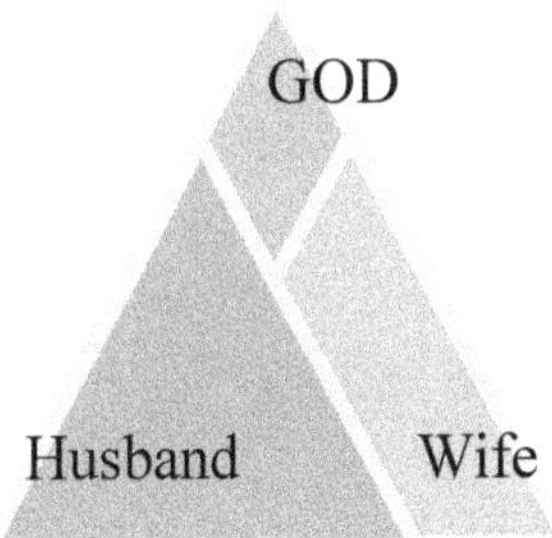

Wherefore they are no more twain, but one flesh. What therefore God hath joined together, let not man put asunder.—Mathew 19:6 (KJV)

God should be the head. You MUST keep him first.

It's not your plan, it's God's plan. It is His divine order for marriages to be rooted in him in order to be successful–both in the good times and the bad times. And trust me, there WILL be bad times.

* Everyday will NOT be blissful

* You will NOT agree on everything

I love to talk to people that are engaged or newlyweds. They are head over heels in love, and they say, *"We have NEVER had an argument or disagreed. We love each other so much!"*

I just smile and say, "keep living."

Adultery Statistics

25-50% of all marriages have experienced an affair

60% of victims are women

40% of victims are men

Disclaimer:

If you are in an abusive relationship –seek help. I say run but that's just my opinion. I am not a doctor and I can't give legal advice. My opinion is you get out. That's just my opinion.

So how do three people become four?

It Happened to Me, It Can Happen to You

One day my world was torn apart. The marriage I thought was "safe," because we both knew the Lord, was challenged.

He cheated and was going to continue to cheat. He wanted out. He said he "fell out of love with me."

What did he say? What does that mean anyway?

I once heard a preacher say you don't FALL in love with anyone. You FALL down the steps, not in love. Personally, I never understood the falling out of love. If you love someone, you love them forever.

Dictionary.com says to fall is:

1. to drop or descend under the force of gravity, as to a lower place through loss or lack of support.

or

2. to come or drop down suddenly to a lower position.

That defiantly doesn't sound like *"falling in love"*.

I thus embarked on my exhausting spiritual battle. The Lord had to guide me, as if I was a child, to totally depend on Him. No matter what happens.

I was taking Jesus 101, Faith 101 & Love 101 all at the same time.

My Prayer

Lord, Help Me To…

____

____

____

____

____

____

____

____

A Woman's Prayer

Lord, I know you are with me and that your Word says you will comfort and guide me. Please give me the strength to do what is right according to your will and your plan for my life. I understand that it is not about me, but all about you. Guide Me Lord!

Notes

Notes

CHAPTER II

YOU CAN'T HANDLE THE TRUTH

Do you remember that famous line from the movie *"A Few Good Men"* with Tom Cruise, Demi Moore & Jack Nicholson?

Just because you want to know, does not mean you need to know.

As women, we love hard, but we also hurt hard. We visualize things. The two of them kissing, holding hands, having sex. That's really very unhealthy. It can cause your mind to replay *"those images"* over and over again. Nevertheless, we think we have to know.

Before voicing all the questions that pop in your mind to ask your spouse, be very sure you can handle the raw and explicit truth. **Just because you want to know, does not mean you need to know.**

We ask those pressing questions; rewinding the tape over and over again in our minds.

"How did this happen?"

"When did it happen?"

"When did he have the time?"

"Did he feel better inside me or inside her?"

"Has she done the things we have done together?"

"How many times did they do it?"

"Is she skinnier than I am?"

"Is she prettier than I am?"

"Did he hold her afterwards?"

The truth sometimes hurts. The answers to these questions are very difficult for a woman to handle. Especially, if the answers are not the answers we want to hear. Nor are these healthy questions to ask, when we are still unsure if we made the right decision to take him back– particularly if we have not totally forgiven him.

Charlie's Angels

Becoming a part of the Charlie's Angels Investigation Team is another no-no. Snooping through phone records, ordering transcripts, checking voicemails and emails are some things we instinctly do. For some, it's just second nature. Even so, we must ask ourselves, can we handle the truth once it is uncovered? To read or listen to explicit details of your husband's affair may be too much for you to handle; and truthfully you don't need that image in your head.

When I first became aware of my husband's affair, I went into Charlie's Angels mode. I was officially part of their team. (I just didn't have a TV show, nor a movie deal.)

Calling numbers back, searching through dirty clothes, looking for the phone, reading the cell phone detail reports, secretly following him in my car, riding around the city, sitting on stakeouts at his job. I truly went too far. Doesn't that sound a bit crazy? Some women want to know, and I was one of them. At least that's what I thought. Nevertheless, what I discovered sickened me. It tortured me. Not the people, but the images and details of the affair. I thought I was strong, but at that time it was too much for me to handle.

Sometimes the less you know, the better. It may save you from backsliding. *(smile)*

A Woman's Prayer

Lord, I know you are with me and that your Word says you will comfort and guide me. Please give me the strength to do what is right according to your will and your plan for my life. I understand that it is not about me, but all about you. Guide Me Lord!

My Prayer

Lord, Help Me To…

Notes

Notes

CHAPTER III

DO I STAY OR WALK AWAY?

Now that the cat was out of the bag, what do I do? Embarrassment and shame had taken up residence in my world. Everyone at the church knew. Family and friends knew. What do I do? I definitely couldn't hide it or make it go away. It was here and we needed to deal with it. To be honest though, I didn't want to deal with it. I just wanted to wake up from this very terrible dream.

> *Love the person – Hate the SIN.*

The decision between staying and walking away is not an easy choice. For me, if I stayed it would require a lot of work. If I walked away, I would be miserable. Despite all the pain I had to endure, I loved my husband. Not the person he became, but the person I married eight years earlier.

Plus there were other factors to consider. There were three innocent children involved; children that hadn't asked to live without a father. They didn't have a choice as to what family they were born into. I felt like such a failure.

No Daddy at Home

Growing up without a father played a huge role in my decision. Not having a father figure in my home was horrible to have to endure. As a child I longed for a father. My daydreams consisted of fairy tales of me thinking I lived like the Brady Bunch. In my imagination, I had both a mother and a father. Marsha, Cindy and Greg were my make believe brothers and sisters. Then reality would kick in, and I would have to accept the fact that it was just a dream. I had no one to call me his little girl; no one to pick me up and swing me around; no one to teach me about boys and what to watch out for. Longing for the love of daddy led me down a road I wanted to shield my girls from.

In making the decision to stay you must ask yourself the following questions, and be honest with yourself.

Self Evaluation

√ Do I sacrifice my happiness just to have their father present?

√ Do I stay with him just so nobody else can have him?

√ Do I just allow the affair and see but don't see?

Absolutely NOT!

Do I want to make my marriage work because I genuinely love my husband and wanted him back?

Most Definitely!

This is an important decision to make. It has nothing to do with anyone else. It's YOUR decision. If your husband has committed adultery, and you are wrestling with whether to stay or walk away, please consider these five tips.

Quiz Yourself

1. Are you sure your reasons to stay are not selfish reasons? E.g., *I don't want him, but I don't want "her" to have him either.*
2. Do you agree to never hold it over his head? E.g., don't continue to throw the affair up in his face – what's done is done.
3. Is this totally YOUR decision? Keep family and friends out of your decision. *(This is your marriage & your family.)*
4. Have you weighed and evaluated the pros and cons? Be honest with yourself. *Are you BOTH willing to do everything in your power to make it work?*
5. Give yourself room for bad days (every day will not be blissful).

List the good and the bad.

Pros	Cons

My Prayer

Lord, Help Me To…

____

____

____

____

____

____

____

____

A Woman's Prayer

Lord, I know you are with me and that your Word says you will comfort and guide me. Please give me the strength to do what is right according to your will and your plan for my life. I understand that it is not about me, but all about you. Guide Me Lord!

Notes

Notes

Notes

CHAPTER IV

THE BLAME GAME

"It's all my fault"

Having to deal with the real issue was not easy. At first I blamed myself. I played the tape over and over in my mind. Where did I go wrong? I asked myself a thousand and one questions beginning with…

"Was I not the wife I was supposed to be?"

"Did I not sex him good enough?"

"Did I work too much?"

"Was I ugly?"

"Was I too fat?"

Will the real issue please stand up

Normally, it has nothing to do with you and everything to do with him. It's about how he feels about himself. Too much pressure, too soon. Bills, kids, work, church…everything comes crashing down. All you talk about is what bills need to be paid, what needs to be fixed in the house or what's going on with the kids. It's not fun anymore. It's too serious.

Most times, affairs happen because the door is opened. By that I mean you allow someone, other than your spouse, to invade your space. The door was opened and now they are in. Have you crossed the line lately? Contrary to what most people believe, affairs begin in the mind. In the beginning, it's an emotional affair. It's sex without penetration. It's a mind thing.

"They understand me."

"We have so much in common."

"We are so good together."

At first it starts with someone just paying attention to the minor details that you have overlooked. We all must count the costs. What is this attention going to cost me in the end?

"It's just a little something, something!"

"I can handle this."

"We're JUST FRIENDS."

Then phone calls, emails and texting begin to become far too frequent. Secrets from each other begin, and then the cell phone is never in the open. It's always out of site–never just charging on the dresser.

"Why is she texting you at 11 O'clock at night?"

"Oh, we're just friends."

Be very careful of just being friends with someone of the opposite sex. Sometimes it is indeed innocent, but it's a dangerous thing to be married and have friends of the opposite sex. You may find yourself sharing more with an outsider than your spouse. Instead, become your husband's ear.

Wives-even if you have no interest in what he is talking about-become interested. Watch the game with him. If you don't understand the sport, ask him to teach you. If you don't, trust me, somebody will.

So whose fault is it?

As women we must stop blaming ourselves for some else's mistakes. Your spouse was grown and old enough to know right from wrong. You didn't hold a gun to his head and make him do anything. And, if he blames you for the choice he made–that's crazy. I don't care what you did or didn't do. At the end of the day we have choices, and whatever choice we make as an individual, they are just that–our choice. If you know you did all you could to make it work, and that you tried your best, then go to sleep in peace. Trying to figure out what you did wrong is not healthy. It's like that recorder playing over and over again, all the shouldas, couldas & wouldas. But, the damage has already been done. Don't try to figure it out. Just move on.

A Woman's Prayer

Lord, I know you are with me and that your Word says you will comfort and guide me. Please give me the strength to do what is right according to your will and your plan for my life. I understand that it is not about me, but all about you. Guide Me Lord!

My Prayer

Lord, Help Me To…

Notes

Notes

Notes

CHAPTER V

THE PROCESS–REBUILDING THE TRUST

I say all the time, *"Taking him back was the easy part. Rebuilding the trust is the hard part."*

On many occasions, I wanted to throw in the towel and give up. It wasn't just work, it was hard work to say the least. There is a process that must take place, and I had to ask myself, *"Do you honestly want to go through the process?"*

When I decided to stay, I knew I was in for a spiritual battle. Most of the battle takes place within, because we are our worst enemy. What I mean is *the mind can play terrible tricks on you if you let it.*

The Enemy Within

Combating the enemy in my mind was exhausting. In the beginning, there was no trust. It was destroyed. Each time my husband was not in my sight, I would get nauseous.

"Was he cheating again?"

"What is he doing?"

"Who is he talking to?"

"Is he really at work?"

> *For God hath not given us the spirit of fear;*
> *but of power, and of love, and of a sound mind.*
> 2 Timothy 1:7 (KJV)

And in case you missed the message…

> *For God hath not given us the spirit of fear;*
> *but of power, and of love, and of a sound mind.*
> 2 Timothy 1:7 (KJV)

Fear and anxiety had the best of me, and I was going under. Those are the times that I would question my decision to stay. This was not a cakewalk. It was not easy and I will warn you, dealing with the real issues, will make you want to run for cover. Many days I said in my mind,

"I can't do this."

"This is too hard."

"I did not sign up for this."

It was torture, but then one day I decided to give it all to God. It was way bigger than me, and what I could deal with. If my marriage was going to work, I had to go to THE source. I had to walk in faith, not on my own ability. I had to have faith to believe that my marriage was GOING to work–no ifs, ands or buts.

One morning I woke up and decided that I was not going to go through this anxiety anymore. I could no longer stand the up days, but mostly down days. Having my heart beating ten times its normal rate and the raging battle in my mind needed to end. So I recited this prayer…

"Lord, I can't be with Jerry 24 hours a day, but I know you and the angels that you have assigned to him can. God, keep my husband in your perfect will. Keep him in all of your ways. I know you didn't bring us back together just for me to be sick and miserable. Lord, watch over him and keep him. If you can't keep him than I guess he just can't be kept! Amen"

That's it; a simple prayer. After that I left it up to God. After all, he was the one in control.

Your spouse must also do everything in his power to reassure you that he is willing to put in the work for your marriage.

Below are six things my husband did and still does to assure me that he is still constantly trying to rebuild the trust.

His Works

1. **Communicate** – Each time he would get in the car, he would call me to talk to me as he drove to his destination. This wasn't necessary, but the fact that he would go the extra mile was in his favor.
2. **Cell Phone** – Leaves the phone out in a public place. This allowed me to take the cell phone with me, if need be. No secrets about phone usage.
3. **Apologize frequently** – In the beginning, he apologized almost every day when he returned home. To apologize just to apologize means NOTHING. His works must back those apologies.
4. **Agreed to get counseling** – This was big thing in my case, as he always said he would never get counseling, but he did. He understood the importance and actually participated.
5. **Reassures me of his love often** – Not just in lip service, but in his actions.

Rebuilding a marriage after an affair is hard work, but it can be done. We did it, and you can too. Marriage is the foundation. It's worth the fight. *I can truly say that today my husband is my best friend, and I am his. It was not like that before. I am thankful for what we had to endure to get to where we are today. You see, not only did we have to deal with the affair; we also had to deal with a child from the affair.*

This topic will be tackled in my next book. Sign up for my newsletter at www.nicoleconline.com and be among the first to get your copy as soon as it becomes available.

A Woman's Prayer

Lord, I know you are with me and that your Word says you will comfort and guide me. Please give me the strength to do what is right according to your will and your plan for my life. I understand that it is not about me, but all about you. Guide Me Lord!

My Prayer

Lord, Help Me To…

Notes

Notes

CHAPTER VI

FINDING ME

In the midst of my pain I found my purpose. This could not have been done without the storm. Every person must carry their own cross—some have several, that's me.

Below is a conversation I had with a sweet elder woman.

The phone rings.

"Hello."

"Hey Baby, I've been meaning to call you."

"Thank you so much for calling."

"Well, I just wanted to share a little of my story with you. You know me and the deacon have been married for over 50 years now."

"Yes, ma'am."

"And it hasn't always been easy."

"I'm sure."

"Well, we've had a lot of bad times and I just want you to know that this happened to me. It happened to me for over thirty years now, and the affair only ended because the other woman died."

"Oh my Lord, are you serious, and you just stayed?"

"Yes, the only time I would see my husband was when the woman was on her cycle."

"What....I'm sorry."

"He would go to work everyday and go right to her house after work. I knew he was there because she lived up the road and my kids would tell me their Daddy's car was there all night."

"But why did you allow it?"

"Because he took care of the house. All I could do back then was domestic work and that wasn't enough to take care of all these kids. So it just went on and on. As I said, it only ended because the woman passed away."

I could feel the rage building up…..or maybe it wasn't rage, it was pain. Pain, for a sweet woman who had to endure so much hurt, pain and shame.

"But, I don't know...wow."

"And when she died he was so depressed. He didn't come out the room for a very long time. And when he did, you

can tell he was mourning. All I can do was comfort him while he mourned her loss."

In my mind I was thinking, "I DON"T THINK SO!" I would not be comforting my very own husband while he mourns the loss of his mistress.

"I'm speechless."

"I'm not telling you to do what I did, it just worked out that way. But you know how to do that computer stuff they do now and you are smart, so you will be ok."

That was the end of the conversation.

Listening to this sweet, gentle woman you could here the embarrassment she carried for all these years. She didn't want to stay, but she felt like she had no other choice. This happens everyday—in the church and outside of it.

This dialogue still haunts me. I used to think about it all day and night.

I believe it also fueled my desire to stand on my own two feet and kick this trial to-the-curb.

For years I was caught up on making sure that my husband was the preacher everyone expected him to be. *Even when he didn't want it.* How it looked to the outside world absorbed me. **Not him.**

What happened to Nicole.

Where did Nicole's dream go?

I knew there was purpose for my life. I just didn't know how to find it or what it was. There were many times I wanted to just call my husband and say, *"Just come home. I will let you continue to see the woman. I just want you back. I don't want to be alone."* But, the love and respect I had for myself was greater than that. The respect I had for my children was greater than that. At that time I had a fourteen-year-old boy, a six-year-old girl, and a newborn. If I allowed my husband's infidelity to continue, my son would think it was okay to treat a woman like this. Even worse, my daughters would grow up thinking this was acceptable behavior for men and the way a woman should expect to be treated. **I DON'T THINK SO.**

At this point something stirred inside of me, feelings that had long been suppressed. I realized I had to take control of my own life. After all, the only person I could change was me.

So, I began to seek God for myself. In the past I have prayed for myself, but not like I prayed for others. My prayer used to be, *"Lord, make my husband the man of God that he is. The man of God that he should be."* Little did I know, that was between God and my husband. Not God and me.

This was when I began to dig deep within me and love me again. I joke that I was in JES 101 and JES 102. But I really was. The Lord was teaching me to love myself despite who says they don't love me—to love myself, despite who walked away—to love myself despite who says they don't want me and I am nothing.

"I will praise thee; for I am fearfully and wonderfully made: marvelous are thy works; and that my soul knoweth right well." (Psalms 139:14 KJV)

This scripture really spoke to me in the midst of the rediscovery of myself. The NIV version says;

"I praise you because I am fearfully and wonderfully made; your works are wonderful, I know that full well." (Psalms 139:14 NIV)

Many nights I would turn to the wall all alone and just weep.

"Lord, why is this happening to me?"

And the response,… *"Why not?"*

It was then that this scripture would come back to me, *"I will praise thee; for I am fearfully and wonderfully made: marvelous are thy works; and that my soul knoweth right well."* (Psalms 139:14 KJV)

This was not about my husband. This was about me loving the God in me. If the Lord made me "fearfully" and he made me "wonderfully" why was I having such a hard time?

Just because my husband walked away, didn't mean God walked away.

These scriptures assure me that he would never abandon me.

"Lo, I am with thee always, even unto the end of the earth." (Mathew 28:20)

"I will never leave thee nor forsake thee." (Hebrews 13:5)

They took root in me.

When my husband first left I blamed myself. I over analyzed everything that was not right about me. I was too black, too fat, didn't cook enough, didn't clean enough. My focus was on me and woe is me, why, why, why?

I was focused on the negative when I should have been paying attention to the positive. When I shifted my focus I began to see what was good about me. I began to see things clearly. The fog began to lift and I began to love again, to breathe again. I came to realize that my good certainly outweighed my bad. This gave me a surge of confidence. After which, my outlook was, *"If he doesn't want me, that's his loss, not mine."* You see, it was not about him. It was all about me.

By the same token, when I began to see the God in me, with all my imperfections, it was easier to see the God in my husband. Despite how he was treating me and how hurt I was, God was still in him.

His mother would always tell me, *"Nicole, love the person, hate the sin. Not because he is my son, but because he belongs to God."*

That took some time, but it did eventually happen. I began to see my husband as God's child and not just someone that hurt me. I began to pray without ceasing for him.

Not for what he had become, but for the God that was in him….it was there. If I could pray for others that called me and for people in the church, why couldn't I pray for the father of my children? I still loved him.

God gently led me through this trial to find the real me again—to fall in love with me again. And I did just that. If I could kiss me I would.

My Prayer

Lord, Help Me To…

____

____

____

____

____

____

____

____

____

A Woman's Prayer

Lord, I know you are with me and that your Word says you will comfort and guide me. Please give me the strength to do what is right according to your will and your plan for my life. I understand that it is not about me, but all about you. Guide Me Lord!

Notes

Notes

CHAPTER VII

IN CLOSING

When you get married no one gives you a marriage tutorial. It's interesting that when you buy a new software program or even a new car, there are all types of instructions, schools, seminars and tutorials. But when you get married or have kids, there is nothing. Yes, Marriage Counseling is in place for those that want it, but it's not mandatory. Why must you have a license to operate a vehicle be a law, but not instructions in how to have a successful marriage before you tie the knot?

Cars and software programs come and go but a marriage is supposed to be for a lifetime. Maybe that's part of the problem. When you get tired of your vehicle and a more updated one is released, you trade that old one in for the new more "advanced "vehicle.

Is that how people treat marriage? Are we always looking for an upgrade? I love my old vehicle. No car payment, no hassle, I know how it operates, and I am used to it. …uuhhmm. Instead of upgrading as a society maybe we should enhance what we already have.

Most think the grass is greener on the other side, but you might find out that it's not even grass, it's temporary grass, an imposter, it's fake–It's actually AstroTurf ™!

I pray this book blessed you.

A Woman's Prayer

Lord, I know you are with me and that your Word says you will comfort and guide me. Please give me the strength to do what is right according to your will and your plan for my life. I understand that it is not about me, but all about you. Guide Me Lord!

In Closing

My Prayer

Lord, Help Me To…

Notes

Notes

Notes

Notes

APPENDIX A: BOOK GROUP DISCUSSION QUESTIONS

1. Do you think Nicole made the right decision to stay?

2. If you were in that position, what choice would you have made?

3. As women, would you agree that we love hard but hurt harder than men?

____

____

____

____

____

____

____

4. What lesson on God's love and forgiveness did you receive from the book?

____

____

____

____

____

____

5. Do women stay for all the wrong reasons?

____

____

____

____

____

____

____

____

6. Do you know someone that stayed and it worked?

____

____

____

____

____

____

7. Do you know someone that stayed and is miserable? What advice would you give them?

____

____

____

____

____

____

8. Was her decision to stay based solely on her not having a father figure in her life?

____

____

____

____

____

____

____

9. When an affair occurs why do women blame themselves?

____

____

____

____

____

____

10. Why was this scripture so important in Nicole's healing? *"I will praise thee; for I am fearfully and wonderfully made."* (Psalms 139:14 KJV)

____

____

____

____

____

____

APPENDIX B: RESOURCES

Appendix

The Holy Bible

Psalms 91 (KJV)

Breathe Again Magazine -
www.breatheagainmagazine.com

Breathe Again's Blog -
www.breatheagainmagazine.com/wordpress

The Plural Thing - www.thepluralthing.com

Money Talk Matters - www.moneytalkmatters.com

Virtual Assistant - www.virtualfreedom4you.com

Business Coach - www.reginabaker.com

The Author's Advantage - www.theauthorsadvantage.com

The Power of a Praying Wife by Stormie Omartian -
www.stormieomartian.com

Sheryl Brady - Don't Lose Your Altar DVD -
www.sherylbrady.com

For more encouragement, I strongly suggest purchasing **Breathe Again Volume 1**. This CD will help get you through the rough moments you may experience in rebuilding your marriage. I have been where you are and would like to share my journey with you.

Breathe Again Volume 1
Purchase Price - $10

Get inspiration from articles such as:

From Pain to Purpose-How I discovered my purpose in the midst of my pain–so can you.

Free From Me-How I had to break free from the battle in my mind.

Never Say Never-How I said I would never take him back if he ever got her pregnant.

My Spiritual Resume-Everyone has a work resume– but what about a spiritual one?

AM I Jealous of My Sister-Have you ever been jealous of another woman?

I also share how I was inspired to write each article.

My prayer is that my writings will be a resource for women all over this world.

AUTHOR BIO

Nicole Cleveland is Chief Editor and Founder of Breathe Again Magazine.

She resides in Norfolk, Virginia with her family.

She is wife to one amazing man and "mom" to three wonderful children that keep her laughing each day. God is Nicole's all in all. He is the steady "rock" that stays consistent in her life. Reading, acting, spending time with her family and "trying" to sing are a few things she loves to do. Nicole is on a mission to ensure women are not "suffering in secret" like she once was, that is why she tells her testimony everywhere she goes. Feel free to contact her at editor@breatheagainmagazine.com and /or visit her website www.nicoleconline.com

To book Nicole for speaking engagements contact info@breatheagain.org or call 757-404-1582

BONUS
WHY DID YOU CHEAT?

My readers kept emailing me wanting to hear why my husband cheated. So I interviewed him and asked the hard question. **"Why Did You Cheat?**

The transcript of the interview follows.

Nicole: Welcome to *Breathe Again Magazine, the Radio Show*. I'm your host, Nicole Cleveland, Chief Editor and Founder of Breathe Again Magazine. We are excited about this show today. My co-host is the love of my life, my friend, my partner, my husband; he is the *"Oodle in my noodle."*

Welcome to the show.

Jerry: Hey, how you doing baby? I didn't understand that *"Oodle in my noodle"* stuff. You gotta clarify that for me.

Nicole: You are truly my *"Oodle in my noodle."* You know…

Jerry: Ok.

Nicole: Today's show is targeted around marriage, particularly my marriage. The pain that we have had to endure and the things we have gone through. Everybody knows that Breathe Again Magazine was birthed out of pain. They understand that it was because you and I went through some things. So, basically this is not a fluff show, at all. I believe people are dealing with some major issues in marriage and marriages are being almost destroyed; well, they are being destroyed.

Jerry: Correct.

Nicole: The divorce rate in the church is higher than it is in the world. So we are going to talk about this thing today, right?

Jerry: Correct. You're absolutely right. I actually feel as though I am glad to be a part of this. I'm glad to see that Breathe Again is actually taking off and it's pretty exciting watching it grow the way it's growing; at a fast pace that it is. You know I never realized how many women are out there that are actually hurting. So yes, I'm very exited for the ministry of Breathe Again and how it is helping so many people.

Nicole: Well great. You know Breathe Again Magazine was birthed out of pain and it was because of you….. so, I'm going to ask the obvious question. All the readers and people I come in contact with want to know the answer to the one big question, "Why did you cheat?"

I just had a baby, we have two other children, we attended church regularly, yet we were traveling down this path. All of a sudden, my world came crumbling down, so can you answer that question? "Why did you do what you did?"

Jerry: I'm pretty sure a lot of readers and a lot of people have come up to you to ask you that question. Pretty much I've been quiet about the whole situation, you know I always tell you it's your testimony, but I think it is time for me to say something; to speak out. The whole reason, basically, is because I was scared, and I was frightened. Bills were getting outrageous. You just had your third baby. You were just… outrageous bills…. and then I got to a point where in ministry-I know a lot of people are saying, *"He was a minister, how could he walk away,"* it was just my way of dealing with pressure.

There was a lot of pressure being a minister. There are a lot of eyes on you, a lot of people looking up to you to be strong and sometimes you'd be surprised at how many ministers, behind closed doors, aren't really as strong as they appear to be.

Nicole: Right. Can we talk about that a little bit, because you say it was the pressures and it was the bills, and it was really overwhelming? However, everybody has bills, so some would say that's not an excuse? You don't cheat because you have bills. So talk about that.

Jerry: Well it really wasn't a way of… the best way I can say this is that my best friend, who is now you, was not my best friend at the time.

Nicole: That's good. That's very good.

Jerry: So the person I was talking to was not you. But, it should have been you, and it's that whole thing about looking for comfort someplace else. And maybe it's because I didn't know how to come to you without being less of a man.

So, there are a lot of men that really, and I want to talk to the men about this, if you sit down and think about this, a lot of men, they fight with this thing called pride.

They don't look at their wife as being their friend. Instead they see where they are not providing, or they aren't doing the man's role. They fear it is going to make them look like less of a man in their wives eyes. And that's not necessarily true. That's something I had to learn the hard way, because when we went through what we went through. If you look toward the end, I had to come back to you anyway and say I'm sorry and let down that wall. And then there was still that wall of pride up there.

Nicole: Do you think pride is one of the major reasons in relationships why marriages are failing?

Jerry: Yes I do believe pride is a major issue. Not only does the man have to learn to say I'm sorry and forgive me and all that. I mean, you know me Boo, you knew I was strong and I had this wall, and even when it comes to my children. I have two girls. So, I have to learn to be more sensitive towards them. I have to learn how to love them, and be a father to them, and also be a man to them. I need to be the one to where, when they come of age, they can say, *"Hey I want a man like my father was,"* and one who will treat them the way a man is suppose to treat them. It's about being a role-model of a man.

I owe it all to Pastor Coward, who came and helped us, and has taught and nurtured me and showed me how to be that husband. Because, it was very hard to open up to you and now it's easy. It's to the point where I can't wait to tell you something.

Nicole: It has something to do with what you said earlier, how I was not your best friend and you couldn't come to before, and it's true. We were so busy; we were too busy doing our own thing. You were going one way and I was going another way. Life just got in the way.

Jerry: Exactly. Now I think I have learned how to appreciate our differences, because I'm not the type of person that'll go out and want to have a business and push myself to do this and do that. I'd rather work my career and what I'm in, but I've learned to appreciate you, as far as you having your business. I've learned to step back and let you do without my manhood being affected.

Nicole: That is good.

Jerry: That is something too. Because there are brothers out there that their wives make more than them, but that doesn't mean you aren't the man. If you are taking care of what you need to take care of at home, then everything else will fall into place, even if she is making more money than you. All this stuff comes down to pride. Once we knock down pride, once we see that our wife is not behind us-but beside us-once we see that our wife is not only our helpmate, but our friend, like they are supposed to be, the first one to know anything that goes on in the house, not somebody outside the circle. Do you know what I'm saying?

Nicole: Do you think that is going on? I think a lot of times men, or husbands, don't feel they can come to their mate so then they look for it in the ears of someone else.

Jerry: Definitely. You have to understand that once you open the door up for the enemy and once you put it out there with your mouth, any problem you have at home and the right ears hear it, then the enemy is going to start playing on your relationship. You'd be surprised how small of a crack he needs to come in. You'll also be surprised that once he's in, how hard it is to get him out.

There are a lot of brothers out there that are having an affair-cheating, and doing all this and running behind their wives back. I had to get to a point where I said, "I cannot afford to do this anymore." Not saying from a financial point of view, not saying for any other reason, but just the peace. I can't afford for my peace to be affected, I have to have peace. When I lay down at night I must have peace.

Nicole: Right.

Jerry: When you are out there, and some of the men are out there, and they are cheating and running here and there, they don't have peace.

Nicole: You didn't have peace when you were out there?

Jerry: No, because you aren't going to have peace when you are wrong. I made the mistake. I was out there and I was doing my thing, there was no peace because I was not lined up with the will of God and I wasn't with who I was supposed to be with.

Nicole: Right.

Jerry: So therefore every time I laid my head down at night there was no peace.

Nicole: You know, I think that is a good point to make, because we know other couples that are going through this right now. What I didn't understand was, if you wanted to come back home, why did you stay away? My thing was, and I have always said, just come back. Was it hard for you to just come back once you left?

Jerry: Yes, I feel as though it is hard to just come back. Even though you said to come back, there was always the fact that I still had to deal with it. I had to deal with the problem. Why I left in the first place.

Nicole: So then my thing is just deal with it. Why is it so hard to deal with it?

Jerry: Because there is also a sense of shame.

Nicole: Ok.

Jerry: There is also a sense of betrayal, because we had kids. At the time our oldest son was like "Wow, Daddy did this to Mom." Then you have to answer all those questions. Then it's that fact of having to deal with it.

Nicole: So, It's easier not to deal with it at all.

Jerry: Exactly, but you know, to me, I feel as though the whole situation was being a coward. That's strong words, but I'm willing to admit that it was actually being a coward and not wanting to face the situation and come back.

Nicole: Right.

Jerry: That's why it took so long to come back.

Nicole: Right. Wow, so we could talk about this all day because we were separated. We were separated, and I thought you had lost your mind. The Bible talks about wrestling against the spirit and the flesh and some people talk about it because they read it, but you and I can talk about it because we went through it.

Jerry: Exactly.

Nicole: It was literally a pulling. You wanted to do good, but evil was present. It was deep.

Jerry: You're right. It's like once you're in, it's so easy to get in, but so hard to get out.

Nicole: That's good.

Jerry: It's an everyday struggle to even guard yourself-and arm yourself. Let me be honest, and let me be real, babe. There are a lot of beautiful women out there. But, let me explain something. There is nobody out there, now that I'm walking with God closer than ever, and that our marriage is the way it is now, for me to give up now. Our relationship is 100% better now, because of the honesty. The reason it is like that is now, I feel and I can speak for you, but every time we have an argument, every time something happens in marriage, God reminds me of what I put you through. So therefore, since he reminds me of what I put you through, that's why I'm the first one to be humble. That's why I'm the first one to come back and apologize, because of the hell I put you through, and because of all the hell I put you through it's a sign of humbleness. Because you to had to go through all that, you deserve to be treated like a queen, which you are.

Nicole: Praise God.

Jerry: Then you know it was necessary if God had to do that for me it was necessary. I believe that it just didn't happen for us and to us for any old reason. I believe there is a distinctive reason why you and I went through this whole situation.

Nicole: Right.

Jerry: While we are actually here to talk about now.

Nicole: Right. So many other people are dealing with this issue and we could go on for days and days and days.

Jerry: It's an ongoing process to rebuild the trust. I'm so glad you brought that up, because there is another thing that the man has to be willing to build that trust and he has to have patience.

Nicole: Yes.

Jerry: While you are going through rebuilding that trust, it's going to take a lot of work.

Nicole: Even in the midst of our separation, when you left you came back three times, to be gone the very next day because it was work to rebuild it. Where are you and what are you doing, and that was work; all the questions.

Jerry: Exactly and you have to be willing to go through that work. Men, if you love her you will go through the work. You are going to go through what it takes to keep her happy and to keep that trust and not have her mind wondering.

Nicole: Right and sometimes you get on my nerves you call me so much, but you know what…

Jerry: I'd rather get on your nerves.

Nicole: I know because I'm so fickle, if you didn't call me I'd be complaining about that.

Jerry: You'd go off on me. You're right about that.

Nicole: But you know what, I thank God for what you've had to endure and what we've went through to have the relationship we have now, because we can't even express how much our relationship has grown and how much I love and respect you.

Jerry: Oh really?

Nicole: Yea.

Jerry: Oh wow, we have to meet in the bedroom tonight.

Nicole: You're so silly. I just love you.

Jerry: I love you too.

Nicole: I thank God that you agreed to do this show and agreeing to do the co-hosting with me about this topic and marriage and infidelity. We are going to take some questions in the future. Is there anything else that you want to say to the women going through this right now about how they can help and not hinder their husband?

Jerry: Well the best thing to do, women, is, and I know it's hard-and I know it's difficult, but the best thing to do is, not nag and not tear them down. Build them up. Even when he is going through this situation, it's tough. The reason why is because you build them up, believe it or not he's listening to what you are saying and by tearing it down makes it easier for him to keep doing what he is doing. But by you building him up and he hears you building him up, it makes it harder to go out and do his dirt because he realizes what he has at home.

Nicole: One last question that I didn't ask you earlier. We talked about how we were in the church and we were busy, busy, busy. When did the fear of God come in there, because I thought all along that you feared God and you would never do anything like this. How did that happen? Where was the fear of God in all of this?

Jerry: To be honest with you I didn't even think about it.

Nicole: Really?

Jerry: I didn't even think about it. That's not saying I don't fear God, it's just that I didn't think about it. That all goes with your personal walk with God.

Nicole: That's good.

Jerry: I mean, look at my walk now and look at me then. Look at my study time now and look at my study time then.

Nicole: Right.

Jerry: My life now and my life back then, you saw material things, and people look at material things as evidence of walking with God. But when you look at me now, you see the material things on top of that you see evidence, spiritually.

Nicole: Right. I tell people all the time, don't let the suit fool you.

Jerry: Exactly. I was fly, I was decked out, I had it all.

Nicole: Yes you did.

Jerry: I had everything. Come on baby you know I had everything. But I'm saying, it was my inner man that was tore up.

Nicole: Yea.

Jerry: I had the outside fixed up good, but it was the inner man that was definitely tore up.

Nicole: Do you think it's important to have a mentor, someone in place to hold your hand and walk with you?

Jerry: To definitely challenge you and to challenge you all the time. One thing that I admire about Pastor Coward is he would ask you how I was treating you. You know I would do my best to treat you good because I wanted you to give him a good report.

Nicole: Right.

Jerry: And not just to say I'm doing that because of him, but he was actually instilling in me how I'm supposed to treat my wife.

Nicole: I think there is a level of accountability there too.

Jerry: Definitely. You need to be held accountable. Exactly. There are some men that may not know how to treat a woman. So you're going to get the ones that are going to say I don't cheat, but let's be real, sex ain't everything.

Nicole: That's right.

Jerry: Sex isn't everything. Just because you are good in bed doesn't mean she's happy the rest of the time because, let's be real, you're only in bed for how long, and then the rest of the time you have to spend time together. So they have to enjoy your company. In order to be satisfied, women are different. My pastor has been teaching me how to be romantic. I try to be more romantic now. I try not to grab you and throw you in the bed all the time.

Nicole: Thank you.

Jerry: You understand what I'm saying, right?

Nicole: Right.

Jerry: You have to be able to have a conversation and keep each other company.

Nicole: Right.

Jerry: I believe that's what Pastor Coward and Pastor Vicki have taught us. To enjoy each other's company. I mean sometimes we sit and talk when we're supposed to be doing something, but we're sitting and talking about something else and we converse and we're so in tune. Now if you look at the way our house is being run now, compared to the way it was then, it's hard for the enemy to sneak in because we are so in tune.

Nicole: Yes.

Jerry: Since we are so in sync, it's just like you know what I'm thinking and I know what you are thinking and we are on the same path.

Nicole: Right.

Jerry: That's what it takes. It takes work. It takes a lot of work.

Nicole: And, it's not easy work, it's hard.

Jerry: Exactly.

Nicole: And I don't want people to think that it's easy and it's not a cake walk. It's work, but its good work. Some work is good work.

Jerry: You are absolutely right.

Nicole: This is good work.

COMING SOON!

IT'S NOT MY FAULT

by Nicole Cleveland

A NOVEL

CHAPTER I

(Excerpt from the upcoming work by Nicole Cleveland)

Work today was stressful. Being in management is no easy task. At first I really enjoyed being a "boss" but as time goes by it seems more like babysitting. Everyday there is a new issue. Someone is calling off, people spending too much time on MySpace, women arguing, it's ridiculous. My kids play better than my staff. Thank God for Jerome and Cecil, our resident male "experts" in the call center. They are the only males that work first shift and sometimes it is a needed relief from all the back stabbing and stupidity that comes from the girls on this shift.

Pulling up in the apartment complex I could see inside my front window. Why was there a group of teenagers in my front room? April knows she can not have company in my house while I am not home. That girl never listens. It doesn't make any sense and I am definitely not in the mood for a shouting match with this chick. She is too grown. It is 6:10 p.m. and I pray she already went to pick her baby brother from the daycare. It closes at six and they have already given me several warnings.

I could hear Lil Wayne blasting from the TV so I'm assuming they were watching videos on MTV or BET. The volume was way too high, yet I didn't understand what he was saying.

I say a little prayer before I attempt to climb the steps to the second floor apartment. *"Lord, please keep me from killing this girl."*

"Hi Ms. Brown," "Hi Ms. Brown," "Hi Ms. Brown."

Each of the teens inside my 700 square foot apartment loudly greets me in perfect harmony. As soon as one said Hi the other said Hi a bit louder. It was then that I realized why they were speaking so loud. April was nowhere in sight and they were warning her.

As if on cue she comes barging out of the bedroom she shares with her brother with some dread lock wearing older young man. Her shorts she had on are way too tight, and definitely too short.

I could feel my blood boiling… the music was giving me a headache and was that a fresh hickey on her yellowing neck?

April went straight for the remote control to turn the volume down.

She gave one of the teenagers a look as if to say, *"Why you didn't tell me my mom was home?"*

All I could say was, *"Where is your brother?"*

"Crap," she said rather loudly. *"I forgot."*

By this time I had exactly 13-minutes to pick him up before they called social services.

This would be the fifth time this has happened and the rules are very clear.

Late more than three times in one month and we call social services. My heart began to race and my pressure began to rise.

"April, please tell your friends to get out of my house."

"It's not a house, it's an apartment, remember we lost our house when you left my dad."

"Just tell them to leave."

April blamed me for everything that happened between her father and me.

Even though he was the one that repeatedly cheated, posed as a preacher and fathered two other children while we were married, by two different women. It was all my fault if you ask April.

And the story begins……

www.ingramcontent.com/pod-product-compliance
Lightning Source LLC
LaVergne TN
LVHW011211080426
835508LV00007B/732

* 9 7 8 0 9 8 2 6 0 0 5 0 4 *